# Bash Command Line Pro Tips

Jason Cannon

# Table of Contents

# About the Author

Jason Cannon started his career as a Unix and Linux System Engineer in 1999. Since that time he has utilized his Linux skills at companies such as Xerox, UPS, Hewlett-Packard, and Amazon.com. Additionally, he has acted as a technical consultant and independent contractor for small to medium businesses.

Jason has professional experience with CentOS, RedHat Enterprise Linux, SUSE Linux Enterprise Server, and Ubuntu. He has used several Linux distributions on personal projects including Debian, Slackware, CrunchBang, and others. In addition to Linux, Jason has experience supporting proprietary Unix operating systems including AIX, HP-UX, and Solaris.

He enjoys teaching others how to use and exploit the power of the Linux operating system and teaches online video training courses at http://www.LinuxTrainingAcademy.com.

## Other Books by the Author

Command Line Kung Fu: Bash Scripting Tricks, Linux Shell Programming Tips, and Bash One-liners

Linux for Beginners: An Introduction to the Linux Operating System and Command Line

The Linux Screenshot Tour Book: An Illustrated Guide to the Most Popular Linux Distributions

# Introduction

As someone that has used the Bash shell almost daily for over 15 years, I've accumulated several command line "tricks" that have saved me time and frustration. *Bash Command Line Pro Tips* is a collection of 10 techniques that you can put to use right away to increase your efficiency at the command line.

# Tip 1: Tab Completion

Using tab completion is one of the easiest ways to increase your efficiency at the command line. Not only can tab completion can save you keystrokes, but it can reveal the possible choices in a given situation. Tab completion can be used to autocomplete file names, directories, commands, arguments, and more.

Let's look at using tab completion to autocomplete commands. After you start typing a command you can hit the Tab key to invoke tab completion. Tab attempts to automatically complete partially typed commands. If there are multiple commands that begin with the string that precedes Tab, those commands will be displayed. You can continue to type and press Tab again. When there is only one possibility remaining, pressing the Tab key will complete the command.

```
# Typing host[Tab][Tab] results in:
$ host
host hostid hostname

# Typing hostn[Tab][Enter] results in:
$ hostname
linuxsvr.company.com
$
```

In this example, you can type a 12 character command with just two keystrokes.

```
# Typing yp[TAB][ENTER] results in:
$ ypdomainname
```

3

```
(none)
$
```

As you can see, tab completion is great for expanding commands. The good news is that it also works on files and directories. For files that start with a common prefix, Tab will expand the common component. For example, if you have two files named file1.txt and file2.txt, typing "cat f[TAB]" will expand the command line to "cat file". You can then continue typing or press Tab twice to list the possible expansions. Typing "cat f[Tab]2[Tab] will expand to "cat file2.txt". After you experiment with tab completion it will soon become second nature.

```
# Typing cat f[Tab] results in:
$ cat file

# Typing: cat f[Tab][Tab][Tab] results in:
$ cat file
file1.txt   file2.txt

# Typing cat f[Tab] 2[Tab][Enter] results
in:
$ cat file2.txt
This is file2!!!
$
```

Here is an example of tab completion with directory names.

```
$ ls -d D*
Desktop   Documents   Downloads

# Typing: cd D[TAB][TAB] results in:
$ cd D
```

```
Desktop/    Documents/ Downloads/

# To autocomplete "Desktop" type "cd
De[TAB][ENTER]"
$ cd Desktop/
$ pwd
/home/jason/Desktop
$
```

Programmable completion is a feature of the bash shell that
allows command arguments to be autocompleted. Not all
command line programs utilize this feature, so your mileage
may vary. For the commands that do use this feature you
can achieve complex command lines with just a few
keystrokes.

To enable programmable completion on an Ubuntu system,
source /etc/bash_completion. You can add this command to
your personal initialization files or you can enable it globally
by uncommenting the the appropriate lines in
/etc/bash.bashrc. The process for other Linux distributions
is very similar.

Let's use autocompletion with the man command to help
speed up our way to the proper documentation we're after.
For example to autocomplete "man subdomain.conf" type
"man subd[TAB]".

```
$ . /etc/bash_completion
# Typing: man sub[TAB][TAB] results in:
$ man sub
subdomain.conf subgid subpage_prot
subscriptions.conf subuid
```

```
# Typing: man subd[TAB] results in:
$ man subdomain.conf
```

This example uses git. By typing "git pu[TAB][TAB]" the only two possible choices are revealed, "pull" and "push."

```
# Typing "git pu[TAB][TAB]" results in:
$ git pu
pull push
```

# Tip 2: Change to the Previous Directory

A quick way to return to your previous directory is to use the "cd -" command.  Your previous working directory is stored in an environment variable named $OLDPWD.  The commands "cd -" and "cd $OLDPWD" are the same.

If you are dealing with fairly long paths and you need to switch between them, using "cd -" makes your life easier.  Since configurations are typically stored in different paths than log files, you can use this technique when you are setting up an application or troubleshooting a problem.  This example demonstrates how to troubleshoot an apache web server configuration  change.

```
jason@linuxsvr:~$ cd /etc/apache2/sites-
available/
jason@linuxsvr:/etc/apache2/sites-
available$ sudo vi wordpress
...
jason@linuxsvr:/etc/apache2/sites-
available$ sudo service apache2 restart
 * Restarting web server apache2
... waiting  [ OK ]
jason@linuxsvr:/etc/apache2/sites-
available$ cd /var/log/apache2/
jason@linuxsvr:/var/log/apache2$ ls
access.log error.log
jason@linuxsvr:/var/log/apache2$ sudo tail
error.log
[Tue Apr 29 20:38:37 2014] [notice]
Apache/2.2.22 (Ubuntu) mod_ssl/2.2.22
```

OpenSSL/1.0.1 configured -- resuming normal
operations
[Tue Apr 01 06:00:01 2014] [error] [client
127.0.0.1] File does not exist:
/var/www/wordpress
[Tue Apr 01 06:00:01 2014] [error] [client
127.0.0.1] File does not exist:
/var/www/wordpress
[Tue Apr 01 06:00:02 2014] [error] [client
127.0.0.1] File does not exist:
/var/www/wordpress
[Tue Apr 01 06:00:02 2014] [error] [client
127.0.0.1] File does not exist:
/var/www/wordpress
[Tue Apr 01 06:00:02 2014] [error] [client
127.0.0.1] File does not exist:
/var/www/wordpress
[Tue Apr 01 06:00:03 2014] [error] [client
127.0.0.1] File does not exist:
/var/www/wordpress
[Tue Apr 01 06:00:03 2014] [error] [client
127.0.0.1] File does not exist:
/var/www/wordpress
[Tue Apr 01 06:00:04 2014] [error] [client
127.0.0.1] File does not exist:
/var/www/wordpress
[Tue Apr 01 06:00:04 2014] [error] [client
127.0.0.1] File does not exist:
/var/www/wordpress
jason@linuxsvr:/var/log/apache2$ cd -
/etc/apache2/sites-available
jason@linuxsvr:/etc/apache2/sites-
available$ sudo vi wordpress
…

# Tip 3: Reuse the Last Item from the Previous Command Line

Many times workflows can revolve around a single item. That item might be a file, a directory, a user, or even something else. Time and time again I find myself needing to run another command against the last item on the previous command line. To access that item in your current command, use "!$".

In this example a file is used to restore some data and is no longer needed.

```
jason@linuxsvr:~$ mkdir restore
jason@linuxsvr:~$ cd !$
cd restore
jason@linuxsvr:~/restore$ unzip
~/Downloads/backup.zip
Archive:  /home/jason/Downloads/backup.zip
  extracting: Documents/cat.jpg
  extracting: Documents/report.txt
jason@linuxsvr:~/restore$ rm !$
rm ~/Downloads/backup.zip
jason@linuxsvr:~/restore$
```

In this example, multiple commands are used to create and configure a user account. After the username is supplied the first time it is recalled on subsequent command lines by using "!$".

```
jason@linuxsvr:~$ sudo useradd -m -s
/bin/bash bob
```

```
jason@linuxsvr:~$ sudo passwd !$
sudo passwd bob
Enter new UNIX password:
Retype new UNIX password:
passwd: password updated successfully
jason@linuxsvr:~$ sudo chage -M 60 !$
sudo chage -M 60 bob
jason@linuxsvr:~$ sudo chage -l !$
sudo chage -l bob
Last password change
      : May 03, 2014
Password expires
      : Jul 02, 2014
Password inactive
      : never
Account expires
      : never
Minimum number of days between password
change          : 0
Maximum number of days between password
change          : 60
Number of days of warning before password
expires    : 7
jason@linuxsvr:~$
```

# Tip 4: Rerun a Command That Starts with a given String

To run the most recent command that begins with a given string, use an exclamation mark followed by that string. For example, to run the last command that started with a "d", type "!d<ENTER>." Specify as much of the string to make it unique. If you have several commands in your recent history that begin with "d", you can add additional characters like "!du" or "!df".

I find myself using this technique to get a status, perform some work that might affect that status, and to recheck the status again. Here is an example where data is being copied to a file system and where the disk usage is being checked.

```
jason@linuxsvr:~$ df -h /data
Filesystem        Size   Used Avail Use%
Mounted on
/dev/sdb1         194M   5.6M  179M    4% /data
jason@linuxsvr:~$ cp backup.tgz /data
jason@linuxsvr:~$ !d
df -h /data
Filesystem        Size   Used Avail Use%
Mounted on
/dev/sdb1         194M   130M   55M   71% /data
jason@linuxsvr:~$
```

This example demonstrates a situation where more than just one character of a string is needed to recall the desired command.

```
jason@linuxsvr:~$ sudo -s
```

```
root@linuxsvr:~# cd /etc/opt
root@linuxsvr:/etc/opt# mkdir myapp
root@linuxsvr:/etc/opt# chown myapp myapp
root@linuxsvr:/etc/opt# chmod 700 myapp
root@linuxsvr:/etc/opt# cd /var/log
root@linuxsvr:/var/log# !m
mkdir myapp
root@linuxsvr:/var/log# !cho
chown myapp myapp
root@linuxsvr:/var/log# !chm
chmod 700 myapp
root@linuxsvr:/var/log#
```

# Tip 5: Command Substitution

If you want to use the output of one command in another command line, use command substitution.  You can perform command substitution by using backticks (`) to surround a command or a dollar sign followed by parenthesis that surround a command.  Surrounding a command with backticks is the older style and is being replaced by the dollar sign syntax.  The output of the command can be used as an argument to another command, to set a variable, or for generating the argument list for a for loop.

This example uses the output of the date command to create a backup copy of a file.

```
$ cd /etc/nginx/
$ sudo cp nginx.conf nginx.conf.$(date +%F)
$ ls nginx.conf*
nginx.conf  nginx.conf.2014-05-03
$
```

This example uses the output of a cat command to check the status of a service.

```
$ cat /var/run/sshd.pid
782
$ ps -fp `cat /var/run/sshd.pid`
UID   PID   PPID  C STIME TTY TIME     CMD
root  782   1     0 11:45 ?   00:00:00
/usr/sbin/sshd -D
$
```

The output of a command can be assigned to a variable and recalled at a later time as in the example.

```
$ ENVIRONMENT=PRODUCTION
$ DIRECTORY=$(echo $ENVIRONMENT | tr
[:upper:][:lower:])
$ echo $ENVIRONMENT | sudo tee -a /etc/motd
$ tail -1 /etc/motd
PRODUCTION
$ sudo mkdir /var/www/$DIRECTORY
$ sudo tar zxf wwwfiles.tgz -C
/var/www/$DIRECTORY
```

# Tip 6: Use a for Loop at the Command Line

```
$ for VAR in LIST
> do
>   # use $VAR
> done
```

When I need to perform the same action for multiple items, I use a for loop right from the command line.  This example loops through a list of user accounts, locks them, and writes a message to the system log file.

```
$ for USER in mike jason chris
> do
>   sudo passwd -l $USER
>   logger -t compromised-user $USER
> done
Locking password for user mike.
passwd: Success
Locking password for user jason.
passwd: Success
Locking password for user chris.
passwd: Success
$ sudo tail -3 /var/log/syslog
Apr  8 19:29:03 linuxserver compromised-
user: mike
Apr  8 19:29:03 linuxserver compromised-
user: jason
Apr  8 19:29:03 linuxserver compromised-
user: chris
$
```

Let's use a for loop in conjunction with command substitution. Note that you can place the entire contents of a for loop on one continuous line.

```
$ for x in $(cut -d: -f1 /etc/passwd); do
groups $x; done
jason : jason sales
bobdjr : sales
jim : jim
. . .
```

You can provide a list of items to the for loop with a variable as in this example.

```
$ USERS=$(cut -d: -f1 /etc/passwd)
$ for USER in $USERS
> do
> echo $USER
> sudo chage -l $USER | grep 'Password
expires'
> done | head
root
Password expires : never
daemon
Password expires : never
bin
Password expires : never
. . .
```

# Tip 7: Rerun the Previous Command with Root Privileges

Since I perform most of my daily activities using a normal user account I sometimes forget to execute a command with root privileges when needed. Luckily it's really easy to repeat the previous command with superuser privileges. If sudo is configured on your system, run sudo !!, otherwise run su - c "!!".

This example demonstrates trying to kill a process that is running as another user. Since that requires root rights, the command fails.

```
$ ps -e | grep nginx
 6139 ?   00:00:00 nginx
 6141 ?   00:00:00 nginx
 6142 ?   00:00:00 nginx
 6143 ?   00:00:00 nginx
 6145 ?   00:00:00 nginx
$ pkill nginx
pkill: killing pid 6139 failed: Operation
not permitted
pkill: killing pid 6141 failed: Operation
not permitted
pkill: killing pid 6142 failed: Operation
not permitted
pkill: killing pid 6143 failed: Operation
not permitted
pkill: killing pid 6145 failed: Operation
not permitted
$ sudo !!
sudo pkill nginx
```

```
$ !ps
ps -e | grep nginx
$
```

This example demonstrates using the su command to repeat
the previous command with root privileges.

```
$ useradd trevor
useradd: Permission denied.
useradd: cannot lock /etc/passwd; try again
later.
$ su -c "!!"
su -c "useradd trevor"
Password:
$ id trevor
uid=1004(trevor) gid=1004(trevor)
groups=1004(trevor)
$
```

# Tip 8: Rerun the Previous Command While Substituting a String

This tip is great for correcting typing mistakes or repeating the same command against different items. To repeat the previous command while substituting a string run "^string1^string2^". This will repeat the previous command using string2 in place of string1.

Here's an example.

```
$ ps -ef | grep nginx | awk '{print $2}'
6809
6810
6811
6812
6814
7992
$ ^nginx^apache^
ps -ef | grep apache | awk '{print $2}'
7912
7915
7916
7996
$
```

By default, only the first occurrence of "string1" is replaced. To replace every occurrence, append ":&".

```
$ grep canon /etc/passwd ; ls -ld
/home/canon
ls: cannot access /home/canon: No such file
or directory
```

```
$ ^canon^cannon^:&
grep cannon /etc/passwd ; ls -ld
/home/cannon
cannon:x:1001:1001::/home/cannon:/bin/sh
drwxr-xr-x 2 cannon ball 4096 Apr  7 00:22
/home/cannon
```

If you do not provide a second string then the first string will be removed from the previous command. Here's an example where an additional "s" was added to a file name.

```
$ cat errors.log
cat: errors.log: No such file or directory
$ ^s^
cat error.log
[Sun May 04 08:43:06.393605 2014]
[mpm_event:notice] [pid 7912:tid
3074292288] AH00489: Apache/2.4.6 (Ubuntu)
configured -- resuming normal operations
[Sun May 04 08:43:06.395060 2014]
[core:notice] [pid 7912:tid 3074292288]
AH00094: Command line: '/usr/sbin/apache2'
$
```

You can omit the trailing caret symbol, except when using ":&".

```
$ grpe jason /etc/passwd
-bash: grpe: command not found
$ ^pe^ep
grep jason /etc/passwd
jason:x:501:501:Jason
Cannon:/home/jason:/bin/bash
$ grep rooty /etc/passwd
```

```
$ ^y
grep root /etc/passwd
root:x:0:0:root:/root:/bin/bash
operator:x:11:0:operator:/root:/sbin/nologi
n
```

# Tip 9: Reuse a Word on the Same Command Line

The "!#" string represents the current command line. To reuse an item on the same command line follow "!#" with ":N" where N is a number representing a word. Word references are zero based, so the first word, which is almost always a command, is :0, the second word, or first argument to the command, is :1, etc.

Here are a couple of examples that demonstrate the use of this technique.

```
$ sudo cp usb_modeswitch.conf !#:2.bak
sudo cp usb_modeswitch.conf
usb_modeswitch.conf.bak
$ ls usb*
usb_modeswitch.conf
usb_modeswitch.conf.bak
```

```
$ mv report.txt $(date +%F)-!#:1
mv report.txt $(date +%F)-report.txt
$ ls *report*
2014-05-04-report.txt
```

# Tip 10: Fix Typos and Shorten Lengthy Commands with Aliases

After repeatedly seeing "command not found" following an attempted grep command, I gave in and created an alias to compensate for my sloppy typing.

```
$ grpe root /etc/passwd
bash: grpe: command not found
$ alias grpe='grep'
$ grpe root /etc/passwd
root:x:0:0:root:/root:/bin/bash
$
```

Note that if you were to log out and log back in, your aliases would be lost. To make them persist between sessions add them to one of your personal initialization files, sometimes called "dot files," like .bash_profile.

```
$ echo "alias grpe='grep'" >>
~/.bash_profile
```

I also create aliases for commands that I use frequently. Even though some of these aren't extremely long or difficult to type, it still saves me time and keystrokes.  Here are my favorite aliases.

```
# Format text into a table
alias ct='column -t'
# Useful for backing up files. Example: cp
hosts hosts.`d`
alias d='date +%F'
# Easy to read df output.
```

```
alias dfc='df -hPT | column -t'
# Quickly resume a screen session or start
one
alias dr='screen -dr || screen'
# Long listing format for ls.
alias ll='ls -l'
# Colorize ls, grep, and tree
alias ls='ls --color=auto'
alias grep='grep --color=auto'
alias egrep='egrep --color=auto'
alias tree='tree -C'
# Time in UTC
alias utc='TZ=UTC date'
# Improved vi.
alias vi='vim'
```

# Conclusion

Thanks for reading *Bash Command Line Pro Tips*. I hope you have picked up at least one tactic that you can start using today to improve your efficiency and effectiveness at the command line.

If you've enjoyed these 10 tips you'll also enjoy *Command Line Kung Fu*. It is packed with dozens of tips and over 100 practical real-world examples.

## Let's stay in touch!

Follow me on Twitter:
https://twitter.com/linuxta

Subscribe to my blog:
http://www.linuxtrainingacademy.com/blog/

Friend me on Facebook:
https://www.facebook.com/linuxtrainingacademy

Subscribe to my Youtube channel:
https://www.youtube.com/user/linuxtrainingacademy

Follow me on Google+:
https://plus.google.com/u/0/116716207503332312214

# Additional Resources Including Exclusive Discounts

For even more resources, visit:
http://www.linuxtrainingacademy.com/resources

**Books**

### Command Line Kung Fu
http://www.linuxtrainingacademy.com/command-line-kung-fu-book

Do you think you have to lock yourself in a basement reading cryptic man pages for months on end in order to have ninja like command line skills? In reality, if you had someone share their most powerful command line tips, tricks, and patterns you'd save yourself a lot of time and frustration. This book does just that.

### Python Programming for Beginners
http://www.linuxtrainingacademy.com/python-programming-for-beginners

If you are interested in learning how to program, or Python specifically, this book is for you. In it you will learn how to install Python, which version to choose, how to prepare your computer for a great experience, and all the computer programming basics you'll need to know to start writing fully functional programs.

### Scrum Essentials
http://www.linuxtrainingacademy.com/scrum-book
This book will provide every team member, manager, and executive with a common understanding of Scrum, a shared vocabulary they can use in applying it, and practical knowledge for deriving maximum value from it.  After

reading Scrum Essentials you will know about scrum roles, sprints, scrum artifacts, and much more.

**Courses**

*Linux for Beginners*
http://www.linuxtrainingacademy.com/lfb-udemy

This is the online video training course based on the book with the same title. This course includes explanations as well as real-world examples on actual Linux systems.

*Learn Linux in 5 Days*
http://www.linuxtrainingacademy.com/linux-in-5-days

Take just 45 minutes a day for the next 5 days and I will teach you exactly what you need to know about the Linux operating system. You'll learn the most important concepts and commands, and I'll even guide you step-by-step through several practical and real-world examples.

*Linux Alternatives to Windows Applications*
http://www.linuxtrainingacademy.com/linux-alternatives

If you ever wanted to try Linux, but were afraid you wouldn't be able to use your favorite software, programs, or applications, take this course.

*LPI Level 1 / Exam 101 Training*
http://www.linuxtrainingacademy.com/lpi-course-1

This course provides interactive step-by-step videos that will help you prepare for the LPIC-1 101 Exam. This exam is important to help you prepare for the Linux+ and LPIC level 1 certification and this course provides all the materials you need to pass the exam.

*LPI Level 1 / Exam 102 Training*

http://www.linuxtrainingacademy.com/lpi-course-2

This course provides interactive, step-by-step videos that will help you prepare for the LPIC-1 102 Exam. This exam is important to help you prepare for the Linux+ and LPIC level 1 certification and this course provides all the materials you need to pass the exam.

### Python for Beginners
http://www.linuxtrainingacademy.com/python-video-course

This comprehensive course covers the basics of Python as well as the more advanced aspects such as debugging and handling files. Enroll in this course to gain access to all 13 chapters of this Python for Beginners course as well as labs and code files.

## Cloud Hosting and VPS (Virtual Private Servers)

### Digital Ocean
http://www.linuxtrainingacademy.com/digitalocean

Simple cloud hosting, built for developers. Deploy an SSD cloud server in just 55 seconds. You can have your own server for as little as $5 a month.

Web Hosting with SSH and Shell Access

### Bluehost
http://www.linuxtrainingacademy.com/bluehost

99% of my websites are hosted on Bluehost. Why? Because it's incredibly easy to use with 1-click automatic WordPress installation and excellent customer service â€" via phone and via chat. I HIGHLY RECOMMEND using Bluehost for your first site. Also, you can use the same hosting account for multiple domains if you plan on creating more websites. Visit http://www.linuxtrainingacademy.com/bluehost to get a special discount off the regular price!

**HostGator**
http://www.linuxtrainingacademy.com/hostgator

If you want an alternative to Bluehost, check out HostGator. It comes with a 99.9% uptime guarantee and includes a free site builder.  They provide customer support 24 hours a day, seven days a week and even provide a 45 day money-back gaurantee.

Made in the USA
Coppell, TX
22 December 2021